THEIR JOURNEY

to the P H D :

*Stories of Personal Perseverance
and Academic Achievement*

THEIR JOURNEY

to the PHD :

*Stories of Personal Perseverance
and Academic Achievement*

SPECIAL EDITION

Edited By

AMINA ABDULLAH, PHD

IP

HAWTHORNE PRESS

MCDONOUGH, GEORGIA

Hawthorne Press
289 Jonesboro Rd
Suite 160
McDonough, GA 30253

First Print Book Edition: October 2014

ISBN-10: 0985431679
ISBN-13: 978-0-9854316-7-9

Library of Congress Control Number: 2014950310

*I dedicate this special edition to my Mom,
Rasheeda El—the biggest supporter of
my academic goals—my role model and inspiration
for taking action and assisting others. Through her
dedication and determination, she has served her family,
brothers, sisters, and community.
Love you, Mom!*

❧

TABLE of CONTENTS

ACKNOWLEDGEMENTS

Special thanks to the numerous women of the PhD Sisters Support Group and to the members of the Pi Eta Delta sorority for their continued support for doctoral students, candidates, and graduates. I am also appreciative of Capella University for their unwavering partnership and support in sharing these stories of graduates from several different universities. This book is a testament to Capella's mission to extend access to high-quality degree programs to adults who seek to maximize their personal and professional potential. Finally, I want to thank the contributing authors for sharing the challenges and triumphs of their journey to the PhD.

Amina Abdullah-Winstead, PhD

Program Lead, Human Services, Saint Leo University

President, Pi Eta Delta Sorority

Founder, PhD Sisters Facebook Support Group

FOREWORD

Each day the news is filled with challenges that need to be addressed. The challenges exist among the young and old, in communities, schools, businesses, and in homes where individuals and families struggle. When I started teaching at Capella University more than a dozen years ago, I knew that many of the graduates would work to help make conditions better by addressing many of the reported challenges. For their dissertations, many would choose significant topics to develop deep expertise, and use their findings to help create change. To date, I do not know how many graduates have gone on to use their research findings, but I do know that Amina Abdullah-Winstead, PhD, has.

I met Dr. Abdullah-Winstead on May 12, 2012, when I stood in the cavernous lobby of the Minneapolis Convention Center to attend the commencement for Capella University. All around me were happy friends, parents, grandparents, siblings, children, and spouses of the graduates. The energy in the space was so warm and positive that we could have kept lights on in the city for a week. I searched the crowd for familiar graduates and found few. Though many of those joyful graduates in their black gowns were unknown, I suddenly heard a voice that I recognized from class conference calls—Craig Winstead, PhD. To my surprise, he was without a cap and gown, which I questioned. He explained that his wife, Dr. Abdullah-Winstead, was graduating the same day. If he had participated in the morning ceremony, it would have been difficult for his family to be ready in the afternoon for the second ceremony, where she would be hooded. I thought what an amazing man, what an amazing woman, and what an awesome couple. Rather than subject the family to the full day of ceremonies, he deferred to her ceremony. This decision helped me to begin to understand just how special Dr. Abdullah-Winstead is as a person, scholar, and practitioner. Her husband cared so much for her that he sat in the audience and watched her march.

Since that day, she has continued to march. Every time she sends me another email, I know that she is marching into the future, modeling the way for others. As a mother and grandmother, she is so disciplined, focused, and committed to growth that she completed her doctoral program and decided to take what she learned and start an academic sorority, The PhD Sisters Support Group, to help other women get the support needed to finish their programs.

Soon after the sorority was established, she showed her genius by collecting the stories of graduates and publishing them. In this collection, each inspirational story reveals pearls of wisdom needed to help researchers complete the PhD journey.

Her compulsion to contribute has not been limited to her network, books, and community service. She also works as a program lead and professor, inviting learners to hallow their lives in purposeful pursuits—giving back. Driven, she is relentless and prolific. The fact that she has prepared yet another book is an indication that she wants more readers like you to actively engage in life's conversations—making decisions and taking action.

I leave you with these final words: Whichever stage in the process you are in, I hope you find the motivation to take the first step, the determination to stay in a course, and the inspiration to finish a dissertation. You just might find that these stories give you hope and reflect your own possibilities.

Rubye Braye, PhD
Wilmington, North Carolina

INTRODUCTION

Their Journey to the PhD: Stories of Personal Perseverance and Academic Achievement is a collection of individual tales of dedication and determination from 11 diverse scholars about their paths to attaining their doctorate degrees. These stories of triumph in the face of numerous challenges can serve as inspiration and motivation to those also seeking a terminal degree. At times, we all face obstacles that temporarily prevent us from achieving our goals. If this is the case as you pursue higher education, allow these stories to serve as a great reminder that all is possible through hard work, commitment, and the support of others who take an interest in your success.

THEIR JOURNEY
to the P H D

1.

MANAGING MYSELF

By Lisa T. Toler

Manager and Project Management Professional (PMP)
Wading River, New York

PhD Organization & Management,
Capella University

MANAGING MYSELF

*Pressure, doubts, and frustration are inevitable
in the PhD process, says Lisa Toler. But the pursuit
of a doctorate is still worth the stress.*

I grew up in a small town on Long Island, the child of an
African-American father and Japanese mother. Because I
had long hair, lighter skin, and almond-shaped eyes, I was
often excluded and teased by other children. My classmates
repeated silly rhythms about eating cheese and…Japanese.
Because World War II still lingered in the memories of many
adults, the teachers didn't encourage me to embrace my Japanese heritage. I learned early not to stand out in a crowd. I
developed into an underachiever.

I went to a community college and received an associate's degree, but I had no clear path in mind about what to do with my life or career. Education was not a priority for me; I had no aspirations of being anything in particular.

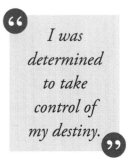

I was determined to take control of my destiny.

At age 26, I found myself pregnant and married to an abusive drug addict. I knew I had to get out of that situation for my own safety, not to mention the safety and well-being of my newborn son. I left my husband and became a single mother. For several years, I struggled to make ends meet, often having to choose between buying groceries and putting gas in my car to get to work. More times than not, I only had enough food to feed my son for the day, and I would go without.

I quickly realized I could not succeed without going back to school. I needed skills and knowledge to find a solid career. Fortunately, I was employed at an organization that offers tuition assistance. Opportunities for distance learning and online education seemed like a good fit for me, so, at age 30, I went back to school for the first time for a four-year undergraduate degree. It wasn't easy—I had a young son to raise, plus a full-time job—but I was determined to take control of my destiny. If I had to sacrifice sleep or socializing to do it, so be it.

Education impacts income

The bachelor's degree I earned helped me land a much better role at work. My salary nearly doubled in a few short years, and I advanced into a new position. The experience of gaining knowledge was rewarding and stimulating. I grew in many ways—psychologically, emotionally, scholastically, and professionally. A few years later, I went back to school to earn a master's degree. Opportunities that I would have never seen without the degrees became available to me, increasing my self-esteem and willingness to assert myself and stand out in the crowd!

Due to my interest in teaching, I decided to pursue a PhD at age 52. I also felt that I could make myself more marketable by obtaining a terminal degree.

I began the doctorate program at Capella University for a PhD in Organization and Management in October 2009. At the time, I was optimistic that I could complete the degree in three years. But you cannot foresee what is going to happen in life: family medical issues consumed much of my first year. It took me four years to finish.

Thank goodness for the support of my friend and husband (I eventually remarried). Without their encouragement, I wouldn't have finished—or it would've taken me far longer to complete the program. Luckily, my husband has a doctorate, so he empathized with what I was going through. He was by my side at every step—especially in the final two years when he could sense that I was feeling overwhelmed.

Eyes wide open

It was certainly challenging. The sense of being inundated and overwhelmed during that period of time was immense. When an adult chooses to go back to school, no matter at what level, he or she has to be prepared to balance studies with work, home life, family needs, and social obligations. You must go into the experience with eyes wide open!

> You must go into the experience with eyes wide open!

Prior to beginning any coursework, I found it helped to share my ambitions and plans with family, friends, and coworkers. The more flexible those around me were, the more it helped me juggle coursework and other responsibilities.

I also set specific days and times during the week when I would complete my coursework and research and tried not to deviate from this schedule. If I did change things up, I forced myself to make up the time. Often, this meant getting up early before work, staying up late, or missing social events. Pressure, stress, doubts, and frustration are bound to appear at this level of learning. However, if you outline a plan early on to mitigate the inevitable, you will succeed.

You need to take time for yourself, too. It may end up being just a few moments a day—to go for a walk or listen to music—but believe me: it will deliver a huge payoff mentally.

Completing the course work, residencies, and the comprehensive exam are not the most challenging factors in this case. What is challenging at this level, however, is writing the proposal and conducting the research. I had never written a proposal before, so the process was extremely difficult. I had to work really hard to achieve a script that was high quality and had my dissertation chair's approval. It took several iterations before I could move forward from this phase. My advice at this stage would be to read the literature on how to prepare a proposal and the university's requirements as much as you can prior to the proposal phase. Also seek the advice of those who have prepared proposals before. Those steps can save you a great deal of time and frustration in the end.

Research that's your own

Conducting the research is actually the most enjoyable and exuberating part in the entire doctoral process. The realization that this is your very own research concept makes it exciting! However, be prepared if things do not go as you first envisioned when preparing your proposal. I experienced several moments during the data collection phase where I had some doubts about my research study due to lack of early responses, and receiving some responses that I had not anticipated.

> *I'm about to get another advancement in my career where I can take on more of a leadership role.*

Putting your findings to paper in a scholarly voice is yet another point that will be demanding and it may not go as you initially planned. You have five grueling chapters in which you can finally flex those scholar/

practitioner muscles to come out the other end as a PhD. The hardest chapter of the dissertation for me to write was the literature review because it can be time-consuming and tedious and is often the longest chapter of all. I kept my eye on the prize knowing the dissertation defense call was right around the corner.

The fulfillment of reaching this goal hit me emotionally the second I completed my dissertation defense call. I am just realizing the benefits of my sacrifices to attain a terminal

I've reinvented myself for the better.

degree at work. The PhD is about to earn me another transformation and advancement in my career where I can take on more of a leadership role. I am excited for the new challenges ahead and the opportunity to grow professionally once again.

Completing my degree has left me feeling like I've reinvented myself for the better. A great sense of accomplishment has emerged from the once bullied, neglected, shy, and introverted underachiever I was. I have a new-found confidence knowing I can achieve my goals and persevere.

If you are reading this and considering entering a program for your terminal degree or are currently enrolled in a doctoral program, know that there are others out there that can help you, have faith in you, and believe that you, too, can persevere.

2.

KEEP MOVING FORWARD

By April Walker

Counselor
Pensacola, Florida

PhD in Human Services,
Capella University

KEEP MOVING FORWARD

The women in April Walker's family believed education was important. But she was the first among them to obtain a terminal degree.

I grew up in a household where education was a priority. It went largely unspoken, but I knew it was my job to go to school and make good grades. The importance and value of education was implanted early in my life as I witnessed my aunt attend college, my mother take courses at a community college, and other family members pursue continuing education classes to enhance their skills and competencies. After seeing their success as a result of continuously learning, I vowed to keep education a big part of my life as well even through obstacles and setbacks.

My educational journey was unpredictable early on. Growing up, I changed schools six times before high school. My stepfather was in the military, so we were constantly uprooted. I resented the military lifestyle because it prevented me from living a normal teenage life. Only later did I realize that moving around so frequently made me resilient: I learned to adjust and make the best of every situation.

My high school years, however, were relatively stable, and I made a priority of hanging out with friends. My grades suffered, but I was comfortable with being an average student and didn't put much thought into my college applications. As such, I was fortunate to be accepted into Bethune-Cookman College to pursue a bachelor's degree.

> *I learned to adjust and make the best of every situation.*

A career-changing class

I chose to major in biology because I was fascinated with becoming a surgeon but, I lacked enthusiasm for math and science and my grades definitely reflected that. Thankfully, at one point, I enrolled in an elective Introduction to Psychology course that piqued my interest. I became intrigued with understanding the science of the mind, and after spending my freshman and sophomore years in biology, I changed my major to psychology. Ever since, I've been infatuated with the study of mental health and felt deeply passionate about advocating for individuals dealing with a mental illness. After four and a half years of school, I graduated with a 3.0 GPA and made the dean's list.

Life happened quickly for me after graduation. I married a man who serves in the U.S. Navy, fully aware of how that lifestyle would affect my life due to the experiences I had as a child. Nevertheless, I was adamant about getting a master's degree and doctorate in counseling. After a few moves and several false starts, I began a school counseling program, very enthused, and was able to complete the two-year program in a little over a year. I wanted to complete the program before we moved again.

The constant upheaval did make me a little discouraged. Still, I was determined to keep pushing while working full time, taking graduate classes full time, and completing the required full-time internship. Then, I got pregnant.

I graduated from the school counseling program with honors, moved to another state, and gave birth to my daughter. My focus had predictably shifted to becoming a parent, but I still wanted to pursue a PhD. Previously, I had only been interested in getting a degree from a brick-and-mortar institution, but I eventually realized that obtaining a terminal degree from this type of school would be relatively difficult given my responsibilities and frequent relocations. A friend who was a military spouse encouraged me to explore online doctoral programs, and while I was initially apprehensive, I soon realized that obtaining a doctoral degree online was the most realistic choice, given my lifestyle. The only other option would be to wait until my husband retired from the military—a decade or more—and quite frankly, that was unacceptable.

Going for the PhD

I began my PhD program in October 2007. I was excited and enthused, even though I had to juggle my studies with being a parent and starting a new job as a school counselor. I did not have a full load of courses right away, so I was able to maintain some balance between work, home, and school. However, as my course load increased, I found myself putting in many late hours, which often caused a considerable amount of stress. Many times, I felt discouraged, but I knew I needed to keep going.

I kept pressing forward and managed to successfully pass each course. Yet, in 2009, I not only became pregnant again, I also was a few months shy of another move. The feeling of defeat began to present itself again because I had not mastered balancing my previous responsibilities and now I was adding another. Being a full-time mommy to an active toddler was demanding and exhausting. I soon realized I needed to reprioritize my life. With a lack of energy to devote to my studies, I had to take a break from school to focus on my upcoming move

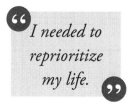

I needed to reprioritize my life.

and the birth of my son.

Being a parent again gave me a new sense of motivation and determination to complete my degree: I was doing it for my children. Though they were young, I wanted them to see the strength and perseverance I had to keep going regardless of the obstacles placed in front of me. And oh, were there obstacles! I entered into a major milestone in my program, which was completing the comprehensive examination. Anxious about tackling this monumental task, I knew I was in a good position to do so as I was fortunate to have the support of my family. I put in a great amount of effort and time into my work and felt confident with what I was able to produce.

To my surprise, however, I did not pass the examination and needed to rewrite one question. Sure of my work, I was certain that I did what was directed and ultimately appealed the grade. Finally, after nearly a quarter, my appeal was approved and I was able to register for my dissertation. I was elated. I began preparing myself for the dissertation.

My dissertation journey was difficult. I went through three mentors, and there were several times when I despaired that I was making no progress. I went through so many emotions including wanting to quit and feeling ashamed. I worried that I was neglecting my family. Despite my spiraling emotions, my family and friends continued to encourage and support me.

Still, I worked hard and managed to stay on track. I tried my hardest not to lose sight of the overall goal in spite of the detours and roadblocks. After 10 months of actively working on my study, I received approval from my committee and was able to successfully defend my dissertation. To hear the words Dr. April Walker left me in

My dream had finally come to fruition.

a state of shock and amazement. My dream had finally come to fruition.

Not easy, but worth it

My journey was never easy, but I know I could not have completed this without God, the support of my family and friends, and my third and final mentor. To see the gleam of pride from my family solidifies that the hard work I put in was not in vain. It was my hope that I was able to show my children that you can achieve a goal no matter how big or small. Perseverance and hard work goes a long way, and my process proves to show that in spite of the challenges I went through, it was these things that successfully pushed me to reach my dream.

It was a dream that filled my heart and mind for many years. I wasn't completely sure of the path I needed to follow to fulfill this dream; however, this journey to a PhD was a road I wanted to travel. Much like an uneven road with many bumps and rough spots, my educational journey was no easy one. There were many times I was uncertain if I would ever reach the light at the end of the tunnel. Nevertheless, through all of life's trials and detours, I was finally able to successfully accomplish one of my major life goals.

This journey reminds me to remain faithful and have patience, as things will work out when they are supposed to. I've put in a tremendous amount of work to get to this point; however, my work is not done. It is my hope that I can be an inspiration to others and provide individuals an extreme sense of confidence to dream and achieve big. Ultimately, no matter the

> *...this journey to a PhD was a road I wanted to travel.*

challenge, demand, or obstacle, keep your eye on the prize and never lose sight of it.

> " *I was finally able to successfully accomplish one of my major life goals.* "

3.

HER FATHER'S FOCUS

By Deanna R. Davis

Student Affairs & College Professor
Oakland, California

PhD in Workforce Development & Organizational Leadership,
University of Nevada Las Vegas

HER FATHER'S FOCUS

*During her PhD studies, Deanna Davis often thought
of her father—who encouraged her to get the
kind of education he was never able to afford.*

Education has always maintained a powerful presence in my life. As a child, I was instilled with its value as the way to a positive, productive life. My father placed such a high emphasis on education that when I was in the third grade, he bought me a chalkboard. As time passed, I began to use this chalkboard to teach the neighborhood children. Even then, I wanted to share my knowledge with others. There was a sense of fulfillment and excitement that came from teaching.

I grew up middle class in the Bay Area. My parents worked hard and expected their three children to do well in school. My father advised me never to receive any grade less than a B, and I made sure that my grades reflected his wishes. Because he had three jobs and often worked the swing shift, I rarely saw him after school. However, whenever I had difficulties with my homework, I would leave the assignment on the kitchen table for him to try to figure out the answers. When I woke up and went into the kitchen each morning, I would find the answers methodically worked out along with an explanation of how my father had solved each problem.

> *There was a sense of fulfillment and excitement that came from teaching.*

My father's parenting left an indelible mark in my life. I learned early on that I wanted to have the kind of strong, dominant persona that my father exhibited. I wanted to emulate his self-confidence, certainty, and ability to influence others. Without realizing it, I was developing an awareness of leadership.

Encountering hate

Growing up, I had never faced any forms of overt racism, but that changed when I left home. My first semester in college, I came back to my dorm room one day and was faced with racial epithets spray-painted on my door. Until that moment, I had been rather oblivious to the severity of racism because I really didn't feel that people could be this mean and cruel. As I reflect back on this experience, I realize this was my catalyst in focusing and embracing my racial identity.

I earned a college degree and entered the corporate world. I also came to realize that the elements of my identity had not included being female and black. Working in corporate America, I began seeing myself through the lens of being a black woman in America. I had been overlooked for several promotions even though I was qualified for each position. When I confronted my supervisor about this, he attempted to pacify me by stating that there would be other opportunities for advancement in the future. I knew that he did not have any intention of promoting me, so I resigned and decided to attend graduate school.

I moved to the East Coast, where I attended New York University, earning a master's in higher-education administration. Returning west, I got a job at a university in Nevada as an academic advisor. A few years into that job, I came under the instruction of a supervisor who became an important role model for me. She was an outstanding leader—intelligent, wise, firm, fair, and adamant about teaching her staff how to be better employees. Prior to her becoming my supervisor, I had never met an individual who, like me, was African-American and who demonstrated as much wisdom as she exhibited. I still model my leadership style on her approach.

In 2006, my supervisor and I met for a routine job evaluation. While discussing my goals for the following year, she indicated that one of my goals would be to pursue a PhD. It was her directive that ultimately pushed me to enroll in a doctoral program, ultimately earning a degree in Workforce Development and Organizational Leadership.

Pursuing a PhD requires some important traits: patience, humility, tenacity, ambition, drive, autonomy, perseverance, determination, passion, focus, resiliency, drive, ethics, and time-management. The hardest part was writing my dissertation. It can be nebulous and daunting to identify your research topic. My topic changed several times before I was able to solidify what I wanted to write about; what I was passionate about. Sometimes, I was able to write fluidly and other times, I left the library without as much as one page written. But I never gave up.

But I never gave up.

Don't do it alone

I deliberately surrounded myself with people who provided me with support and encouragement. It's important to find folks who are in your cohort with whom you can study and write. You may have to distance yourself from friends who want to hang out and have you participate in things that will take you away from your studies. In the beginning, I tried to keep my social life active, but soon realized that I had to refrain from going out as much. Even when I did go out, I would feel guilty because I knew that I should be studying or writing. You have to find balance, as well as manage your time.

I deliberately surrounded myself with people who provided me with support and encouragement.

One thing that I realized on this this journey was that I could not do it alone. I decided to start a support group with women who were also enrolled in a doctoral program at the university. We met monthly to dine, vent, and lift one another's spirits. We all felt that we needed to lean on one another just to endure this process. Some of us were married; others were in relationships and had children. We all discussed our struggles in having to juggle all of it. We all realized that we were at the mercy of our faculty chair and dissertation committee members.

> " *I could not do it alone.* "

I had difficulty being humble and allowing my chair to direct my research. I felt that it was my research, and I wanted to control what I studied. That is rarely the case in PhD programs, however. My chair and committee members basically told me what type of qualitative design I should follow and how I should analyze my data. There were times when I wanted to challenge my chair, of course, but this would have been detrimental to my completion. Therefore, I learned the important characteristic of humility. There were times when I felt like dropping out due to the pressure.

My program required 60 credits of coursework and 12 dissertation credits. Since I attended school part time, it took me three years to complete my coursework. After completing my coursework, the program required that we have oral comprehensive exams. After passing my comprehensive exams, I was able to register for my prospectus course. In prospectus, we were expected to complete our first three chapters. My life revolved around writing on a daily basis.

My research study brought out my real passion. I sought to explore the leadership development experiences of African-American women as they ascended to senior leadership roles in academia and business. The academic literature was largely bereft of how race and gender informed leadership development. As a black female, I was most interested in the leadership development experiences that helped catapult the participants into senior leadership roles. After three years of coursework and

> *My research study brought out my real passion.*

two years writing my dissertation, I graduated in December 2012 with my PhD.

Believe it to achieve it

Currently, I serve as the Director for Academic Enrichment at the University of Nevada Las Vegas (UNLV). I also teach part-time at UNLV in the doctoral program in workforce development and organizational leadership. I enjoy working in higher education and plan to continue working as an administrator and college professor. My commitment to higher learning

> *After completing my doctoral degree, my self-confidence has intensified.*

and my experience have helped to clarify my determination to educate and assist others. Higher education has been, and will continue to be, the avenue through which I will conduct my work.

My advice for anyone who is enrolled in a doctoral program is to keep your eyes on the prize. One should never give up; stay focused on earning your doctoral degree. If you can believe it, you can achieve it. After completing my doctoral degree, my self-confidence has intensified. I was able to complete a goal that was one of the most difficult challenges that I had ever experienced. The path to obtaining my PhD was truly a journey. It was a journey that I relish and would not have changed. I accomplished a goal that my ancestors, parents, and life prepared me for. It was a journey that I believe was a testament to God's plan for my life.

One of the hardest things for me to face when I earned my degree was the fact that my father would not be there to see me graduate. He passed away in 2003, and I went through a difficult time adjusting to life without him. He had played such an instrumental part of my life that I could not imagine being without him.

The day after I finished defending my dissertation, I had to write my dedication page. This was truly one of the most difficult pages for me to write. My dissertation was dedicated to my parents and the unconditional love and support they had provided me. Tears welled up in my eyes as I wrote the dedication, because all I could think of was how much I missed my dad and wished he was there to see his baby girl graduate with a doctoral degree.

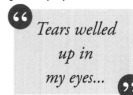

Tears welled up in my eyes...

4.

REACH FOR THE SKIES

By Doraine Baul-Pinson

Licensed Independent Mental Health Practitioner
Omaha, Nebraska

PhD in Human Services – Counseling,
Capella University

REACH FOR THE SKIES

*Doraine Baul-Pinson quit college to
join the Air Force. But her desire to grow
and learn ultimately led her back to academia.*

My father was in the military, so I grew up on Air Force bases in Georgia, California, and eventually the Midwest. By the time I graduated from high school, I had average grades and absolutely no clue about my future. Many of my friends either enrolled in college, or joined the military.

I qualified for a scholarship at a nearby university and enrolled. But like many students who are first in their family to attend college, I struggled academically and eventually found myself on academic probation so I decided to leave college and join the Air Force myself.

In fact, the Air Force provided me with some much-needed discipline, as well as the maturity to handle grown-up responsibilities. I became more confident, developed concrete goals, and cultivated a sense of ambition. I decided to return to college.

By then, I had gotten married and had two children in diapers. Unlike my first attempt, I would not be returning to college as a single person without responsibilities. I had a family, and a full-time career, so I knew I had to be on point. Before I made an appointment with an academic counselor, I needed to examine why I failed my first attempt at college. I felt embarrassed about flunking out, but I believed that by sitting down and reassessing what led to failure, I could correct those faults and succeed. After developing my list, I came up with some workable corrections. I resolved to:

- ☐ Read the assignments and do the homework on time
- ☐ Sit in the front or at least close to the front (I used to sit in the back)
- ☐ Take notes during the lecture

I committed to making those changes, and while they may sound simple, they were the things I had previously failed to do.

Learning from failure

I reentered my academic pursuit slowly, taking two evening courses. It was difficult juggling family and academic responsibilities, but I did well, and I even ended up on the dean's list. I still got frightened about failing, but in hindsight, I often learned more when I failed at something than when I did well. When I fail, I sit

> *I often learned more when I failed at something than when I did well.*

back and reflect on why. Facing my failures enables me to be realistic about myself and my abilities, but at the same time challenges me to look at what I can do to avoid the failure. I have found that mentally preparing for something can often assist in achieving the goal.

During this time, I also had to contend with an extremely difficult situation. My husband had begun using

> *Facing my failures enables me to be realistic about myself and my abilities...*

crack cocaine, and he developed an intense addiction. He began draining money from our accounts, and even from my student loans. He had a great deal of guilt, and it was not long before he checked himself into a rehabilitation program. But he dropped out a week later, returned home, and resumed his drug use.

By then, I had begun my senior year in college and found myself struggling with another problem: the remaining classes I needed were scheduled during the day when I was at work. After doing some checking, I learned of an Air Force program called Bootstrap, which would allow me to attend college full time without reporting to duty, while still receiving

> " *I applied and was thrilled to be accepted.* "

my full military pay. In return, I had to agree to enter officer's school, and any additional training if an opening in my degree appeared, and I would give them back two years for the one that I needed to attend school full time. I applied and was thrilled to be accepted

"I just kept moving"

During my senior year, my husband's addiction grew worse, and his actions forced me into a rigorous schedule. My day began at 4:30 in the morning when I woke the kids and drove a half hour to my in-laws. From there I went to school and worked at one of my internships. As a journalism student, I interned at a local television station, worked production at the university studio, and wrote for the college paper. My day usually ended around 6 p.m., and I retrieved the children and began preparing for the next day. People ask me how I accomplished all of that, and I always say, "I don't know. I was on automatic, and I just kept moving."

I eventually graduated—still on the dean's list—with my bachelor's in journalism, and returned to my military career. At the time, they did not have any officer openings in my field, so I went back to my regular job as a supply clerk. I had orders to Korea for a year, and I could not bring my family. I left my children with my parents.

Once I arrived in Korea, I began looking into master's programs. The installation offered two programs, one in business and one in human relations. I enrolled in human relations, and found graduate work to be both intense and gratifying. I also became curious about the process of obtaining a doctoral degree. A professor explained that the process generally took five years, and when everyone gasped he said, "Well look at it this way, you can attend school for five years and get a doctoral degree or you can just live five years and be five years older." When he put it that way I thought, "Well, the former seems like a plan."

> *Well look at it this way, you can attend school for five years and get a doctoral degree or you can just live five years and be five years older.*

Back to America

When I returned to the states, my husband was clean, and he had retrieved our children from my parents. He accepted a job, and he was working on a drug and alcohol degree. I kept the children, and he and I worked out visitation and other issues. I also performed my internship, made the decision to separate from active duty and join the Air Force Reserve. Once I left the Air Force, I had a difficult time finding work. My children and I moved in with my parents. I worked many low-paying jobs, but eventually I got better work. My husband and I also decided to try to work on our marriage, but it was difficult to bridge the distance between us. We eventually separated.

I found a job working as a therapist and decided to

pursue a PhD online. My schedule involved getting up around 8 a.m. in order to do household responsibilities, go to the gym, and be at the office by 11 to see clients. I usually finished at the office around 5 or 6 p.m., went home, ate dinner, and began my graduate work at 8. I was often up until 2 or even 3 a.m. I was tired, but I was determined. During this time, I was dating another man, who had moved in with me. He often took the children to school and assisted me around the house by cooking and cleaning. He eventually became my husband.

I took the summers off from learning until I began working on my dissertation. I put together a study based on my work experience. I often had child welfare cases, and I was amazed at the mountain of work and the challenges associated with working those cases. I felt the mental health field could improve in this area, and I also felt it was important that families stay together whenever possible. I was especially interested in families where one or more parent suffered from a mental illness. I began collecting articles on the subject early during my doctoral education.

Becoming a scholar

My doctoral journey was actually quite similar to how the professor in my master's program described it. I had my idea based primarily on the cases I worked. Many of them involved child welfare cases. I worked with parents and families who had a history of abuse and neglect, and who had lost custody of their children. I wanted to research ways for professionals to successfully reunite families whenever feasibly possible. I had to find theories that supported child development, families, and communities to provide a basis for my inquiry. I then had to develop a study in which to obtain data and answer the question of which counseling interventions worked for families involved in therapy as one requirement of the court system.

I talked to several professionals who shared with me their success rate, their struggles, and their overall experiences with these cases. I found the process lengthy and sometimes tedious. When I look back at my academic journey, I admit there were many times when I wanted to quit. I made it through with the help of my husband, my family, and even my first husband. Eventually, I finally went through the stages of doing academic work and had demonstrated my ability as a scholar. I still have a great deal to learn in this area, but I'm pleased with my success.

In July 2012, I marked graduation with a celebration that included family members and friends. I felt proud, excited, and thrilled that my parents were able to share this occasion. A few months later, I received a certificate that stated, "Doctor of Philosophy in Human Services with a specialization in Counseling Studies." Since that day, I have been on another journey where I am trying to define myself as an academic professional and working on setting new goals.

I believe life is a journey we all take, and I have often presented it that way to those I taught in courses or workshops. I often encourage my participants to savor and celebrate the milestones of a good grade, a successful final project, or even a quiz as they travel their own academic journey as I did on mine.

5.

JUST DO IT

By Kenya Goodson

Environmental Consultant
Hyattsville, Maryland

PhD of Philosophy - Civil Engineering,
University of Alabama

JUST DO IT

*When a friend told her to stop talking and start doing,
Kenya Goodson decided to take the plunge
and pursue a PhD in chemical engineering.*

I am grateful to have received education beyond high school. My mother and grandmother—neither of whom got a college degree—raised me. Even though we lived in poverty and spent most of my childhood in housing projects or sub-par housing, I was able to get an education because they made sacrifices to support our family.

I did not have friends in junior high school. High school was when I started developing friends. It was also the first time that I was in an environment that didn't punish kids who were smart. I really enjoyed my high school years, despite some discouraging feedback.

I did exceptionally well in chemistry and took an advanced-placement chemistry in the 11th grade. I liked the class, but it was also my first encounter with racism. One day, my chemistry teacher asked me what college I planned to attend. I had not really looked at any schools, but when I told her what institutions were writing me, she made a statement that I never forgot. "Those schools are a little steep for you," she said. I was in shock. I determined that day to prove her wrong.

What next?

I graduated high school with honors and attended Stillman College on a tuition scholarship. My father, who reentered my life when I was in my teens, was admissions director at Stillman and helped me get a scholarship. Those years shaped me into the person that I am; I developed a sense of scholarship and pride as a black woman. I forged long-lasting relationships with great people. I worked on my first research project. I flew in an airplane for the first time to present my research in Washington, D.C. I became a member of Delta Sigma Theta, working in the community doing public service. But I did not know where I wanted to go in life. What was God's plan for me? What next?

After graduation, I could not find a job that fit my skills. Furthermore, I didn't really know what I wanted to do. I worked customer service at the Tuscaloosa Kmart. I was miserable. After four months, I quit and went to work at Stillman as a Resident Hall Manager. I hated that even more. After lots of prayer and introspection, I realized I desired a career where I could use my science background to work with people. I was broke, but I enrolled in the master's program for environmental management at Samford University, got a degree in environmental management, and eventually landed a job as a public health environmentalist in Alabama.

I enjoyed the job, which involved inspecting private sanitary septic systems and the soils in which they are installed. I met land surveyors, geologists, and civil engineers. I negotiated with land developers, septic tank installers, homeowners, and businessmen. But after four years, I decided that I wanted a different career. I also believed that there was more to life than what I was doing, and I wanted to do work that was significant and impactful. As such, going back to school seemed like the right thing to do.

With my chemistry background, I had several options including toxicology, engineering, public health, and many more. I decided to try engineering because I figured I would be able to solve major environmental issues. When I told a professor at the University of Alabama (UA) that I was interested in getting a master's in environmental engineering, she said, "Why don't you go for a PhD?" I thought she was crazy. Me, an engineering PhD? But everyone said the same thing.

> *I also believed that there was more to life than what I was doing, and I wanted to do work that was significant and impactful.*

I couldn't decide. I talked and talked about it. Finally, one of my friends told me she was tired of me talking about it. She said, "Just do it and stop talking about it!" I was offended, but provoked in a powerful way to make a change. I applied to the PhD program and started at UA in the fall of 2005.

Naiveté—and racism

My PhD experience was interesting. I didn't have anyone advising me on how the process went, and I didn't have a particular research area on which to focus. I just wanted to *save the world*. Since I did not have a bachelor's in engineering, I had to take undergraduate prerequisites and graduate courses at the same time. I also worked as a graduate assistant with Engineering Student Services and served as a mentor to minority students.

> *Why don't you go for a PhD?" I thought she was crazy. Me, an engineering PhD? But everyone said the same thing.*

Black engineering students had interesting experiences with their white colleagues at UA. The program is mostly white, and some did not want to team with black students, which set a dangerous precedent for the workplace. Engineering is a team effort and it is inevitable that teams will be assigned on a project. In the beginning, I felt very alone.

As far as my research was concerned, I had no idea what I was doing. I would meet with my professor to discuss what I had done, but I'd exaggerate my progress week after week. So, when the rubber hit the road, my advisor blew a gasket. The "progress" that I made was nothing like a paper. I didn't know what a paper was supposed to look like.

We parted ways and I found a new advisor who welcomed me and gave me the specifics on the project that I was to be working on. My first thought was, "I thought I chose what to work on." Ignorance is a terrible characteristic to have when you are a PhD student. I had to work on a project of which I had no knowledge or passion. It was hard to stay motivated. My first assignment was to develop a literature review for the project. I asked myself, "What the heck is a literature review?" It's a good thing I can laugh about it now!

Two years into the project, my funding was cut. I had some animosity. I really did. My chair felt bad for me, but I was not sure how much of it was in his hands. It was an administrative decision. He also told me how he appreciated that I worked on the project in spite of how I was treated. I really believed that my funding was cut so that I would quit the program, but I had no intention of dropping out. They would have to kick me out. I worked on that project for two years without funding, until my chair pulled some strings and I received money again.

I finally figured out what a decent paper looked like and started going to conferences and presenting papers. I began to take ownership of my project

> *Ignorance is a terrible characteristic to have when you are a PhD student.*

and my dissertation. I became more confident in what I was doing. I understood how the project worked with my undergraduate background. After passing my prelims and defending my proposal, I became a candidate.

Little sleep, much success

I was given a timeline to defend and submit my manuscript. I don't think that I got any sleep for four months. The data were analyzed and submitted. I was working on my dissertation day and night. I woke up thinking about my dissertation, and I went to sleep thinking about it. I went to lunch with computer in tow. I didn't get any sleep the night before the deadline. I was so scared of the big, bad dissertation defense. All of my committee members, including my chair, seemed gleeful that afternoon as I defended. And my mom was there.

I passed and felt great. My committee told me what revisions I needed to make and I began making them. But it was harder than I thought. It was not content as much as it was structuring the manuscript for submission. The table of contents made me cry. I had to add figures and tables to my table of contents—and I had a lot of both. I was working day and night again! When I finally submitted my manuscript, a huge weight lifted off me. When the manuscript was approved, I was a PhD.

To my surprise, I was also the first black woman to receive a PhD in chemical

> **When the manuscript was approved, I was a PhD.**

engineering in my program at my school. I never would have known that, except a friend told me. I didn't believe her at first, but after graduation, I made some calls and discovered the Department of Civil, Construction and Environmental Engineering had just one African-American female PhD—that's me! I'm still in disbelief.

> *To my surprise, I was also the first black woman to receive a PhD in Chemical Engineering in my program...*

6.

REALIZE YOUR OWN DREAM

By Quentin Newhouse Jr.

Experimental Social Psychologist and Executive and
Core Performance Dynamics Specialist Coach
Montreal, Quebec, Canada

PhD Experimental Social Psychology,
Howard University

REALIZE YOUR OWN DREAM

*Quentin Newhouse Jr.'s decision to pursue a
PhD was inspired in part by
Martin Luther King's famous "I Have a Dream" speech.*

A chievement has always been important to me. Whenever possible, I have sought to make the most I can of the gifts I have. Perhaps because of my parents' influence— neither of them have college degrees—I have long valued education.

I went to kindergarten the first year that the Washington, D.C., public school system was desegregated. Looking back, I think I learned to believe that I could achieve anything because I attended school with everyone.

My parents put a priority on learning and were willing to make sacrifices to ensure that I got the education I needed. When I was 10, they decided to move the family uptown from living in my grandparents' house. The schools in our new neighborhood were better and the streets were safer. I knew the names of all of my secondary school teachers. (I had the privilege of participating in one of my first public speaking engagements roughly 25 years later when I was asked to give the retirement speech for my second grade teacher.)

> *I have long valued education.*

In high school, I was a moderately popular. I was also a C student, the president of a fraternity, and clarinet player in the marching band. In August 1963, I attended Dr. Martin Luther King's "I Have a Dream" speech, which made me want to make a difference in the lives of others. I decided to become a doctor and enrolled at Marietta College, a school in Ohio, where I was one of 20 black students in a student body of 2,000. I intended to be a math major, but my Fs in freshman calculus suggested I was unlikely to succeed. I was put on academic probation and began to wonder whether my dreams of even getting a college degree were feasible. I decided that I needed to find another major if I ever hoped to become a doctor. But I made a pact with myself that I would never give up. Against the odds, I would pursue my dreams.

Working hard

The assassination of Dr. King on April 4, 1968, during my sophomore year, had a huge impact on the nation and on me. I rededicated myself to fulfilling his dreams through my professional career. I settled upon a psychology major, and after graduating, decided that I wanted to pursue graduate training in the field.

Given that my overall grade point average was C plus and my graduate record examinations scores were average, I was not sure what would happen. I prayed that where there was a will, there would be a way. I applied to 10 schools and was not accepted by any of them. My first choice was Howard University. Howard University's doctoral program was started in 1958 and was known for producing one to two doctorates in psychology each year. I wrote the college a letter stating that they made a mistake in not admitting me. Soon thereafter, I received a telephone call to come discuss this matter with them. After two hours of being questioned on the topic of psychology by a panel of four professors, they admitted that perhaps they had made a mistake and provisionally admitted me.

Other graduate students made fun of me because I had a penchant for reading everything and always volunteering when a professor asked for volunteers. I read every volume of the Handbook of Social Psychology and could actually quote sections, theories, and authors. I studied very hard and missed many things occurring in life because of my focus on my graduate studies.

An additional and remarkable footnote is that my dissertation committee chair left the university before I completed my paper. Normally, that is academic death; however, the department chair stepped in and assured me that I would finish under his tutelage. In 1980, I graduated with a PhD in experimental social psychology. I was only 30 years old.

The joy of teaching

Throughout my career, I have been fired twice, demoted once, and left several jobs I perceived to be dead ends. I have always been marketable, and am grateful to have been resilient enough to work in so many diverse settings. I have taught at the university level since 1976. I love to stand in front of a group of eager, inquisitive students who are waiting to learn what I have prepared for them. I have taught at more than 10 universities, for almost 40 years and for six years online.

At age 50, I relocated to Tennessee. Not having the appropriate contacts, I had a friend drive me to all the local universities. I was able to teach several part-time courses at Tennessee State University and at another school. Eventually, I discovered Strayer University, where I interviewed for a part-time teaching position. I was told that since the university focused on business and accounting courses, I could never work there full time. For two years, I accepted the occasional Introduction to Psychology, Social Psychology, and Introduction

> "Throughout my career, I have been fired twice, demoted once, and left several jobs I perceived to be dead ends."

to Sociology courses and was just happy to be teaching.

Eventually, I became dean and, under two years of my leadership, the campus and faculty increased in size and won a Most Improved Campus Award.

In 2011, I moved to Canada and decided to reinvent myself. I realized that I wanted to serve people in another capacity. Coaching was gaining credibility and I entered an eight-month certification program. My wife encouraged me, as I had to travel to Toronto and Chicago for labor-intensive work. I am certified in several areas, including with the International Coaching Federation. I opened a successful Executive and Life Coaching practice in Canada with clients in America, Canada, Australia, and Thailand. I have made several presentations and workshops, including a presentation to the National Basketball Retired Players Association and to 140 Conference Montreal.

My journey is not bad for a C student in high school and college who was rejected by 10 graduate schools or a person whose parents and grandparents were not college educated. God deserves all the credit for my achievements. But I also believe you should never give up or abandon your dreams. All of your dreams can be realized if you consider alternate realities, reinvent yourself, and adapt what you are doing when it does not suit you or serve you.

...never give up or abandon your dreams.

.

7.

PROVE THE EXPERTS WRONG

By Cheryl D. Jackson-Golden

Department Chair – Social & Behavioral Sciences
Pine Bluff, Arkansas

PhD in Human Services,
Capella University

PROVE THE EXPERTS WRONG

Almost no one believed Cheryl D. Jackson-Golden could suceed in obtaining a PhD. But she did.

would probably not be writing about my journey as a PhD sister if I had listened to the messages I got from the world while growing up:

- ☐ "You're not college material."
- ☐ "Your ACT scores aren't high enough"
- ☐ "The work is too hard. The bar is too high for you."

Fortunately, I didn't pay any attention to those messages—and I succeeded.

Neither of my parents had a college degree, and I didn't obtain mine until midway through adulthood, after getting married, having kids, getting divorced, and remarrying. Entering college as a nontraditional student was challenging, but I had support.

> *Fortunately, I didn't pay any attention to those messages—and I succeeded.*

I had volunteered in Service to America with a local nonprofit agency that provided services to low-income families in the Delta of Arkansas. I was lucky, blessed, and fortunate to secure a full-time position as a trainer, earning livable wages with benefits for me and my children. The executive director was a great supervisor and motivator, and she insisted that I enroll in college full time. "The company will support you, so there is no excuse. Schedule your classes as needed. We will help you with childcare."

Moving fast

In my undergraduate program, I studied social work. My work experience and course work mimicked each other, making the classroom experience enlightening. After receiving the undergraduate degree, I continued work in service delivery during the period of welfare reform. I worked full time, traveled out of state frequently for my job, had teenagers, and succeeded in getting a master's in three years.

I remarried in 2006, and quickly became bored because my husband's job caused him to relocate and to return home only for weekends and holidays. Now teaching adjunct and working as the training coordinator for a local long-term care facility, I was quickly learning the culture of higher education. My husband suggested I go back to school and get a PhD. Of course, the first thing that went through my head was "Smart people get those, and I am not smart." But he began to help me search for programs that were suitable for my needs. I considered several programs, but Capella University best suited my needs. I began my program in the spring of 2009 and my degree was conferred in December 2013. My degree has been totally supported through student loans and personal employment income as needed.

An instructor that early on had said, "I do not know how you made it this far" became a support for me, because he fueled me enough to seek the assistance to succeed. Colleagues and associates were cordial and occasionally inquired about my success in the program. My department chair offered support as requested, along with one additional senior faculty member from the college.

Initially, my children, along with my husband, had no clue of the work required; often questioning the long hours thinking, writing, reading, and then crashing as the quarter ended. The most significant highlights from my years of study includes: (1) joining the PhD Sisters, (2) a computer crash during the summer of 2012 when I had a total meltdown, (3) hanging out with other doctoral learners at the residencies.

Looking back, I have been most fortunate in having had daily housekeeping services during the past eight years. I have no children residing at home now, and my husband has never required or demanded much of my time. During my daughter's junior year of college she became pregnant, so I had to readjust my life and thought processes related to time management to help raise our granddaughter. A year after entering the doctoral studies program my husband joined me at Capella working toward his doctoral degree. We are truly believers in education. Two of our four children are in graduate programs and one in undergraduate studies.

Learn to say no

Since obtaining my doctoral degree, I received a promotion to department chair in February 2014 and continue to teach adjunct for another for-profit university. If I had to share lessons to current learners or those contemplating seeking a terminal degree, I would say make sure that it is truly your goal and that you are willing to embrace it in that manner. Be prepared to readjust your life and at times to say to the world, "No, I have to study and write." My husband and I had many study dates; study weekends, a time to meet for meals, worship, and bedtime.

Set realistic goals for yourself and your life related to your responsibilities. Do not overload yourself with

> *Be prepared to readjust your life and at times to say to the world, 'No, I have to study and write.'*

classwork, and track your available financial aid resources. It takes an enormous amount of time for research. Residencies (class, travel, hotel, food) are not financed—meaning you cannot rely on school funds. Try to catch sessions close to home to not set yourself back financially—save for those sessions, if possible. For the comprehensive exam, if possible, clear your calendar for at least two weeks. No weddings, vacations, extra duties; no guests, girlfriend conversations, or procrastination. Listen to your mentor and follow instructions. I had class-mates who could not understand how I finished at such a rate. I listen well. I'm always writing or researching something. Find an editor that is familiar with writing styles, grammar, other writing mechanics, and then invest. Build a network of individuals with similar goals.

My dissertation research was fueled by my continued curiosity about women who are intrigued with the desire to attain a college degree in spite of the numerous barriers that they often face. Being a professor for many years, and before this time a trainer in an employment training program, I heard many stories. Sometimes, I didn't even hear them, I simply observed them. But those stories of women who succeeded against the odds inspired me because I was once one of those women.

8.

A PATH THAT WOULD PLEASE HER MOTHER

By Andrea Little Mason

Sustainability Specialist
Hampton, Virginia

PhD in Educational Leadership – Curriculum & Instruction,
University of Phoenix

A PATH THAT WOULD
PLEASE HER MOTHER

Andrea Mason's mother was a lifelong educator—
an inspiration that ultimately led her daughter
to pursue a master's and PhD.

always admired my mother, Johnnie Mae Gray Little. A
native of Alabama, she was the first in her family to finish
high school and attend college. She earned a degree in
biology and went on to get a master's in computer science.
She taught math and computer science for 28 years, and both
she and my father were deeply involved in educational efforts
throughout our community. I also saw my mother as a model
example of *every woman*. I desired to be like her as a wife,
mother, educator, and servant. She influenced many people's

lives and my goal was to exemplify the kind of finer woman that she was.

My mother passed away in 1994, three months before my college graduation from Tuskegee University, at a time when I did not yet feel equipped to navigate womanhood as a wife or mother. Newly graduated and newly married, I found myself becoming bitter about my life and relationships. I wasn't following my mother's example. But at my lowest point, I decided to stop mourning my loss and to begin celebrating her legacy. I decided to expand upon the work my mother had done as an educator. I knew that the work ultimately began with working on me as an individual.

In 1996, I earned a master's degree and began teaching in the public school system. But ultimately I made a decision to homeschool my children. I spent more than a decade of satisfaction and fulfillment being consumed by homeschooling my four sons. I enjoyed every moment of it, and then I began to realize something was changing in me. I had many opportunities to work with individuals in their relationships. All of this ultimately led my husband and me to establish a successful nonprofit based on relationship education. From these experiences, I desired to advance my expertise in this area.

The online option

As I watched others soar through their careers and be promoted to higher heights, I felt stuck in the ashes of my former life where my previous professional aspirations no longer seemed relevant. This is where the University of Phoenix entered my situation. I had been contemplating pursuing a terminal degree for a few years and knew it was the right time for me to begin. However, I knew that a

" I felt stuck in the ashes of my former life. "

traditional university was not suitable because extensive travel was not an option for me.

A PhD seemed like a mark of excellence and the right way to pursue the kind of research and teaching I wanted to explore. I have always been a project-oriented individual and viewed my doctoral process as an extended project that would last for several years. I completed the coursework and dissertation over an uninterrupted four-year period.

However, learning online presented some challenges for me. Initially, there were hurdles I had to overcome as a communicator. In online environments, everything that your peers know about you is based on how adept you are at communicating in the learning forum. I was strongest in my verbal communication skills, and while I also communicated well in writing, I became more aware of the importance of tone in my communications. Learning how to communicate with a team in a virtual setting was one of the greatest gifts I received from my doctoral process. I have also become more effective in my other personal and professional relationships as well.

I began my program in November 2009, and completed it in October 2013. University of Phoenix has an integrated program, so I was able to begin research for my dissertation in the summer of 2011. I submitted my dissertation proposal on the last day of my final content course in December 2013.

Diving deep into a topic

My dissertation was titled "Non-Conventional Gender Roles in Relationship Education Curricula for African Americans: A Content Analysis." The results of the study confirmed the misalignment between relationship curricula designed for African-Americans and African-Americans' actual experiences. Further, the results of the study showed that the foundational principles of the sample relationship education programs were based on traditional contexts of relationships that do not accommodate the changes in women's roles in society. These findings have since been used to develop curricula that address personal and professional relationships in a context based on equality, equity, and respect.

As I encountered professors and scholars, literally from all over the world, I have felt myself regenerate. At the University of Phoenix, I was able to connect with a great leader in relationship education. While building my dissertation committee, she reached out to me and offered to guide me through my dissertation process. As few others could, she introduced me to the entire field of relationship education, so that I could find the topics of interest to me and narrow my interest to a single topic that I could base my dissertation research on.

It wasn't easy getting through the process. I had to resubmit my proposal twice before I received the quality review and Institutional Review Board (IRB) approvals. Over the next three months, I made recommended revisions to my proposal and received the necessary approvals to begin collecting data. I received IRB approval in March 2013. After completing data collection and data analysis and writing my results, I submitted my dissertation to my committee for final review during the last week of June 2013. I was the first person from my cohort to finish the doctoral process and successfully completed my oral defense in August 2013.

Thankfully, I had an enormous amount of support from my spouse and my sons while pursuing my PhD. My husband, Eugene, and I recognized that roles would need to change for every member in our home. In addition to functioning as a family, we were committed to working as a team. We also recognized that there would be areas where we would need to cheat on our regular responsibilities. Regardless of the how we teamed up, adding my doctoral process to our household meant that some things would not be able to be done as they had been in the past.

Challenges and companionship

I confess I felt guilty about my effectiveness as a wife and mother during this period. Until this point, I had always been available for my children and they were accustomed to being my only commitment. Beginning the doctoral program changed what my role looked like in my home. Some people suggested that my having a doctorate while my husband had only bachelor's degree would be detrimental to my marriage. Both Eugene and I made the necessary adjustment to ensure that our relationship remained strong and continued to grow. Additionally, Eugene was inspired by my academic success. He is completing an MBA in sustainability.

Friendships were particularly challenging to navigate. Many could not understand my focus and lack of a social life. I knew there would be friends who would transition out of my life and others that would travel with me during the doctoral process. I also understood that my academic pursuits would expose me to new people and opportunities. I was determined to embrace the journey throughout the process. What a journey—a rewarding one—it has been!

What a journey—a rewarding one—it has been!

Advice to Others on Their Doctoral Journey

- ☐ Do not be afraid of change! It is a part of growth during the doctoral journey.

- ☐ Do not expect that life will ever get back to normal after completion of your program. Your life will forever be changed.

- ☐ Get accustomed to reading literature on a regular basis.

- ☐ Learn about and become associated with professional organizations in your field.

- ☐ Begin to attend conferences in your field so that you can network.

- ☐ Make opportunities to write after you have read the literature.

- ☐ Allow your mind opportunities to synthesize the

information you have just read with the information you already knew.

☐ Learn APA format (or whatever formatting your university uses) and practice using it during your content classes.

☐ Use the tools available through Adobe Reader; Control F will be your best friend as you sift through the research and articles to find relevant topics and supporting content.

☐ Get connected with others working on their doctoral degrees through social media.

☐ Embrace the journey and become the expert!

9.

ADOPTING NEW HABITS

By Jaqueline "Jacque" Eaves

Life Coach & Career Advisor
Woodbridge, Virginia

PhD in Human Services – Counseling,
Capella University

ADOPTING NEW HABITS

*Jaqueline "Jacque" Eaves navigated the PhD process
while adopting two children—which added
to her own research on the topic.*

I grew up in a military family and spent much of my childhood in Little Rock, Arkansas. The city was the site of the first school desegregation battle in the 1950s, which was indeed a blessing because even though my family wasn't well-to-do, I ended up at a school with some of the most affluent residents. Students from middle- and upper-class families surrounded me. My parents encouraged me to become involved in every club and organization possible to increase my exposure to different experiences and opportunities for obtaining scholarships for college.

I was an average student. I would study all evening for a test and get a C, whereas my sister would skim over the material and get an A. My mother quickly identified my struggle and encouraged me to stay in those books. That encouragement was vital.

I loved sports, but I was not athletic. I attempted basketball, but ultimately settled for a position as the team manager. I maintained the game stats, filled water bottles, and carried basketballs. I loved being around the game and this afforded me a front row seat. I also figured if I was going to be on the bench I could make good use of the time. This experience taught me humility. I also saw how coaches encouraged, directed, and inspired a team. The value added to each player was priceless.

As high school drew to a close, I applied for the colleges in Arkansas that were affordable and was content with choosing the first school that accepted me. One of the colleges I applied for was Henderson State University (HSU). After receiving admission to HSU, I initially wanted to major in psychology, with a minor in business, because I had aspirations of having my own private practice. But after struggling in my accounting and economics courses, I quickly changed my major to sociology.

Relocation, relocation, relocation

I graduated in May 1995 and, after a long search, got a job with the leading communications provider in Little Rock, working as a customer-service representative for the mobile phone division. During that time, I began falling in love with a man I met in college; he was the man of my dreams. He swept me off my feet by flying me around town in his plane for dinner dates. Two years later, we married. Our wedding was everything I dreamed of, and we were surrounded by family and friends. We moved Texas, where my husband was training to be a Navy pilot, and then to Virginia, the first in a series of transfers.

I enrolled in a master's program at Norfolk State University in an Urban Education: Guidance and Counseling program. I knew that I did not want a clinical career path and that I did not have the time to devote to hundreds of hours of supervision, as I did not know where my husband's job would take us next. I enjoyed the practical approach to my education and learning applicable information in the human services field. I graduated with a master's degree in 2001.

I went to work at a well-paying job at a leading human service agency. I provided therapeutic intervention and services for children at risk of removal from the home due to their behavior in the home, school, and/or community. I met amazing, talented children and teens. I also met traumatized and confused ones. Having seen the other side of residential treatment, I enjoyed the prevention part of treatment much more.

Choosing adoption

Around this time, I learned that I would need fertility treatments to conceive a child. However, the treatments and frequent deployments do not mix well when timing is everything. After considerable emotional pain and yet another relocation, my husband and I decided to pursue adoption. Within one week to the day of completing our required foster parent classes, we received a call that a little girl was born and in need of a home placement. The vetting process was long and daunting with frequent home visits and court hearings. Finally, at a ceremony at the courthouse on National Adoption Day, we became the parents of a beautiful baby girl. I was in awe of the number of African-American children present at the ceremony and stunned by the lack of African-American adoptive families. I felt compelled to do something; I just did not know what.

One year later, we moved to Japan. Living overseas was a turning point in my life. My husband was out to sea more than 75 percent of the time. I made the most of the time by taking an active role with my sorority, spending quality time with my daughter, and praying and seeking guidance for my life. I was frustrated with restarting my career with each move.

> *I felt compelled to do something; I just did not know what.*

My husband and I began brainstorming next steps. I knew I wanted a PhD, and an online program seemed best for me as it afforded me the flexibility and offered the challenge I needed for this season in my life. I enrolled in a doctoral program.

The time came for us to transition back to the United States. I was going a hundred miles a minute trying to ensure that I stayed on top of course room requirements and deadlines. I emailed my instructors to let them know that I was traveling internationally and would make every effort to stay on top of assignments. I boarded a flight from Narita International in Tokyo bound for Chicago with textbooks and our four-year-old daughter in tow. My husband was on a different flight because he had to return to finish his tour.

Three days later, I woke up in the hospital. I had suffered an inflight emergency: meningitis, rooted in complications from a previous sinus surgery and compounded by altitude. I was required to stay there for 10 days to continue medication regimen. My life changed forever. I learned to pay attention to my body and to maintain a sense of balance.

Embracing parenthood

We settled into our new home in northern Virginia and my studies continued. I got a job at a human services agency providing services to homeless children and families. My work with the homeless population often required night hours, a conflict with my values as a parent. I wanted to be home to feed my family and put my daughter to bed. The stress of work, family, and school began to take its toll. As much as I struggled to maintain balance, I knew that something had to change especially with the date for the comprehensive exam was approaching.

> " *My life changed forever.* "

I passed comprehensive exams and began to explore a possible thesis for study. I was encouraged to pursue a study that could sustain my interest long-term. At the time, my husband and I were in the process of adopting a second child—a boy—and I was shocked by the disproportionate number of African-Americans in foster care and available for adoption. I began the task of narrowing the topic to something that would add to the body of literature on the topic.

My dissertation chair was also my mentor and he was a wonderful supporter and guide throughout the process. He challenged me and kept me accountable throughout the journey, even when the tasks grew more difficult. The introduction of the scientific merit review slowed my progress (it took almost a year to obtain the needed signatures to proceed with the study). It also took me a while to locate a church in a second state where I could conduct research.

The week of my dissertation defense, I received a call from the adoption agency that had helped us find both our children. The social workers wanted to know if we would consider a possible placement of a biological sibling for one of our children. It forced my husband and me to determine if we would include another child in our family (we ultimately decided against it), but most important, it reminded me that the study was indeed relevant. The need for foster adoptive homes remains. I set up alerts in my email of news articles related to my topic to keep me abreast of the latest information.

The day before my defense, I received an article that my state successfully placed more than 1,000 foster children in adoptive homes, due in part, to a social media awareness campaign. This was the evidence that I needed to support the Adoption Awareness Theory that emerged from the study. In

2013, I graduated from Capella University with a PhD in Human Services. While my life has not been perfect, I am blessed and able to say that it is filled with purpose. Every challenge that I have faced has led me closer to where I am supposed to be in this journey called life. I will continue to advocate for children in foster care awaiting adoption and grow my business as I help others realize and reach their goals. I thank God for wisdom and understanding!

> *Every challenge that I have faced has led me closer to where I am supposed to be in this journey called life.*

10.

UPS AND DOWNS

By Demetria M. Hill Cannady

Mental Health Counselor
Valdosta, Georgia

PhD in Human Services – Counseling,
Capella University

UPS AND DOWNS

*It wasn't all smooth sailing for PhD candidate Demetria Hill.
But ultimately she got the degree—
and career direction—that she wanted.*

Growing up, I always knew that education was important even though no one in my family emphasized learning. I got good grades that could have been much better had I applied myself. I was the student that did enough to get by, especially in social studies, science, and math. In elementary and middle school, I recall being an A or B student. As I approached high school, my grades were all over the place. I didn't really care as long as I didn't fail any courses. However, I do recall receiving an F in social studies because I didn't pay attention. And history was boring to me.

It was my high school math teacher who made the biggest difference in my early education. She invested time and energy into making sure that I understood what she was teaching. When I did not understand, she gave me extra assistance and tutored me until I did. She instilled some values regarding life and the importance of being an educated African-American female. As a senior getting ready to graduate from high school, I really began to think about my future and attending college. Prior to that, I really had no idea of what I wanted to do with my life. I knew I wanted to leave home, and I really wasn't ready to work for minimum wage, and definitely was not going in the military, so I think college became my only option.

I decided to attend a historically black college, Fort Valley State, in Georgia. Fort Valley was close enough to home if an emergency happened, yet far enough away so that my parents wouldn't drop in on me. I began college in 1991 as a business major and ended up obtaining a bachelor's in social work. While taking business courses, I realized that business was not what I wanted to do. So I began to take courses in education, psychology, and social work. Social work became my major of choice after completing an internship at the mental health center in the substance abuse unit. At that point, I realized that I enjoyed helping people and could identify with some of the situations that these people were in and had been through.

Juggling kids and education

In 1996, I enrolled in a master's program for mental health counseling. I became pregnant with my first child, but wanted to complete the program after I gave birth. I had to make a decision either to remain in Fort Valley and place her in day care with people that I did not know, or move home to have assistance from my family. Soon thereafter, there were four deaths in our immediate family, so this helped me to decide to move back home to Boston, Georgia. I still had a year to complete in my master's program, which meant that I had to intern for at least 600 hours and I had two or three classes left (not online classes). Fort Valley was a two-and-a-half-hour drive from where I lived, so in order to achieve and obtain this degree, I had to do some extraordinary work. I met all the graduation requirements including passing the comprehensive exam in July 1999.

I started my first job as a graduate in August 1999, working as a social services director for a residential intermediate care facility for mentally handicapped individuals. I enjoyed the job, but it was not challenging. One day I was asked if I'd ever thought about pursuing a PhD. I said, "What for? Nobody's going to want to pay me for it." I had not thought about returning to school because I was comfortable with my position and my salary.

But that conversation got me thinking. I changed jobs, had children, left the workforce, and then decided to return. But no one was willing to hire me in my field, so I decided to enroll in school to obtain a PhD. I had all this free time, why not use it? I called and spoke with an enrollment counselor at Capella University and was told that I could take a course to see if I could adapt to going to school online, and if so, I would be enrolled in January in the PhD program. I started my first PhD course in December 2007.

I took a full course load of PhD classes with no breaks. I began and completed my comprehensive exam during the summer quarter in 2010 and was excited to finally move on to working on my dissertation. I sent my topic to my mentor and she stated that this was a good topic, and she was excited to see what comes next. Approximately two weeks later, I was told that I was assigned a new mentor because a hand injury had made her unable to fulfill her duties.

Difficult dynamics

My new mentor immediately challenged me in regard to my dissertation topic. I had to approach the study a different way, or I had to completely choose another topic. I was devastated because I'd been collecting articles for the past three years and was ready to write my dissertation and get it done. On the other hand, I understood she was only looking out for me and my academic success. After pouting for a few days, I re-grouped and began to approach my study regarding attachment from a different angle.

During the last week of the quarter, I sent my mentor a list of new topics that I thought might work. She agreed to a topic on parenting styles and I officially began my dissertation process. However, my mentor and I realized our working styles weren't compatible. We agreed that it would be more beneficial to me and my journey if I found a new mentor, again.

I began sending emails to potential mentors and eventually connected with a new Capella instructor. I asked her if she would be willing to take me on as a new mentee. She stated that she would like to speak with me on the telephone. I emailed her a copy of my completed scientific merit review to see if this was a topic of interest to her. She agreed to become my mentor and we began working together in September 2012. She stated that she would do whatever needed to be done to get me completed as soon as possible as I had been in the dissertation process far too long. I thanked her and cried after I got off the telephone with her. I was finally feeling as though I would make it to the end of the dissertation process. Within a year, I had reached the final milestone thanks to the support of my new mentor during the transition and the dissertation process.

Worth the hard work

In addition, I had the support of some strong and educated women from the PhD Sisters and other groups who were very supportive. When I was on the path to throw in the towel, they reminded me that I'd come too far to quit. Also, I was grateful to receive assistance and that I was able to offer assistance to other women/sisters who were having some of the same difficulties that I'd experienced with the stress of family, mentors, employment,

> *When I was on the path to throw in the towel, they reminded me that I'd come too far to quit.*

and dissertation. When no one appeared to understand, these women knew exactly what I was experiencing and were able to encourage me from that position.

The PhD process taught me a lot about myself. I would like to think that I have given my children a prime and personal example of persistence, endurance, and the ability to never giving up until you have achieved your desired goals. While completing my dissertation, I attended most parent meetings and activities at the school, if I didn't forget them, and became an active Boy Scout parent. I sometimes feel bad that we weren't able to vacation because I was writing and researching and/or the finances did not allow. But I have vowed since then to make up some missed talks and vacations that we lost. The moral of the story is you can do anything you put your mind to. I thought it, I dreamed it, and I achieved it.

I've always been told that you must work hard for anything worth having. I can truly say that my PhD was not given to me, and I definitely worked hard for it. I sacrificed a lot of money, family time, outings, and clear thoughts. I can say that I had to re-learn what it means to relax. I'm still working on that!

> " ...you must work hard for anything worth having. "

11.

SURVIVAL STRATEGIES

By Thomasine T. Wortham

Psychotheripist
Portsmouth, Virginia

PhD in Human Services – Counseling,
Capella University

SURVIVAL STRATEGIES

*Midway through her doctoral studies,
Thomasine T. Wortham faced a battle with cancer—
and won.*

I grew up in the slums of Portsmouth, Virginia, and during childhood, I carried some level of shame about our house, which had an outdoor bathroom despite the fact that we lived in the city. Still, I never allowed the shame to stop me from having friends or from being involved in a variety of activities. I volunteered for school and community projects, and Mama always had a program for me to be involved in at church. Somehow, I never internalized the message that I was poor and never felt underprivileged.

Growing up during the 1950s and 1960s in Virginia meant living a segregated life. There were white and colored neighborhoods, bathrooms, lunch counters, waiting rooms, water fountains, movie theaters, and the like. Of course, there were exceptions, but the general climate reflected a separate, and definitely not equal, philosophy. These realities changed externally with the enactment of the Civil Rights Act of 1964. But legislation does not change hearts. Until that time, we observed the boundaries that parents taught us at an early age. I remember when my friend next door and I were both 16 and went job hunting. We were so excited about the possibility of getting a job, in a department store or other business environment. At that time race appeared on employment applications, and it dawned on us that once we checked Negro, we might not be contacted. Amazingly, my peers and I were not bitter, angry, or resentful of these experiences. They only made us more determined to succeed.

I attended Catholic school until I completed fifth grade, when I convinced my mother to allow me to attend public school. My all-important reason was that I did not want to wear uniforms, which would be required when I entered sixth grade. Surprisingly, my mother granted my request. Her

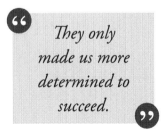

They only made us more determined to succeed.

acquiescence paid off, as I was a great student, and was quite advanced when I entered public school.

High school was a place where I flourished, serving as captain of the cheerleading squad, editor of the yearbook, and homecoming queen. Thanks to my wonderfully supportive teachers and guidance counselors, I received scholarships and loans for college, attending Norfolk State University. I maintained a work-study job and sometimes a job off campus as well, usually with a class load of at least 16 credit hours. Determination was a necessary attribute, because I often used public transportation, requiring three bus changes, to get to class.

From mom to therapist

Shortly after college graduation, I joined my husband who was a Special Forces Green Beret Officer in the U.S. Army. As an Army officer's wife, I experienced tremendous growth, met people from all over the world, and gave birth to two wonderful sons, Tracy and Darren. We lived in Fort Bragg, North Carolina, and enjoyed that period of our lives. Most of the time in North Carolina, I was a stay-at-home mom; however, I entered the workforce as a teacher's aide for a brief period before our family relocated to Flint, Michigan.

The adjustment to living in a new place was significant. Along with the major climate change, came the need to learn the culture—fast paced and demanding. Additionally, we moved to an area where few African-Americans lived. My son Tracy, now in kindergarten was one of a handful of African-American children in his elementary school. The process of finding daycare for Tracy and Darren required a great deal of emotional work on my part. I was in a strange place with no family and far away from friends. Amazingly, we all acclimated to the change, but as the years wore on, multiple stressors caused deterioration in the marriage.

In 1988, my spouse and I separated. About a year later, he filed for divorce, and the marriage ended after 19 years. Divorce was the last thing I ever wanted my children to experience; however, that was the reality. I continued to reassess my life and embarked upon a career change, pursuing a Master of Social Work degree from Michigan State University. The MSW program was therapeutic and a tremendous help during my healing process. During this season, I sought therapy, a decision that I place among my best choices. I was determined to heal, and I was committed to becoming as whole as possible for myself, my children, and for the clients that I would serve. I completed the MSW program in 1990, entered the human services field as a substance abuse counselor, and later became a clinical social worker. In 1994, I started my private practice, Grace Counseling Services, a Christian counseling practice.

Tested in many ways

In September 2009, I officially began the journey at Capella University to pursue a doctoral degree in Human Services with a specialization in Counseling Studies. Though tentative about e-learning because of my love for face-to-face interaction, I nonetheless forged ahead. My new husband (I remarried in 1991), had received bachelor's and master's degrees online, and I had observed firsthand the commitment, sacrifice, and discipline involved in the process.

I describe this PhD journey as an exceptional time of growth and expansion. My coursework at Capella was enjoyable, and I loved the online format, much to my surprise. With all of the travel that we did for my husband's business, I was able to complete assignments on airplanes, in hotels, and countless other places not possible with traditional learning platforms. I excelled in coursework, despite numerous challenges and crises, which is true for most, if not all, doctoral learners. However, my greatest battle was yet to come.

This battle, more like a monster, began to rear its head at the end of my final course in December 2011. Shortly after I submitted the final 50-page course project, I was diagnosed with early stage breast cancer. The priorities in my life changed immediately.

There were countless decisions to make from this point forward, such as whether to proceed with the comprehensive examination, which medical tests to undergo, what treatment protocol to follow, which surgery to have, and whether to put the whole PhD process on hold. Academic advising encouraged me to take a break and care for my health, but my medical team advised moving forward and going on with my life. My husband, children, extended family, and friends voiced support 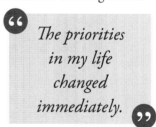 of whatever I chose to do. Finally, after a great deal of prayer, I decided to move forward with the comprehensive examination.

There was one upside. Between the multiple medical procedures and the grueling comprehensive exam period, I had the opportunity to mature in an important spiritual discipline: patience.

The priorities in my life changed immediately.

After completing my comprehensive exam, my status changed from learner to researcher, which felt wonderful. More decisions lay ahead, choosing a mentor, committee members, medical decisions, and many more. During this period, I began a medical protocol for the early stage breast cancer and officially entered the dissertation phase.

In June 2012, I had yet another screening, and this time it was good news. The MRI detected no cancer cells. We rejoiced and thanked God, but we still faced decisions about surgery and radiation treatments because of the precancerous cells and calcification that were detected in previous biopsies and screenings. I was blessed with the benefits of early diagnosis before any tumors or masses formed. In addition, my oncologist and surgeon advocated for me to use an alternative treatment, a tiny but extremely powerful daily pill, rather than chemotherapy. I felt fine all along and continued the major undertaking to obtain my PhD.

> *...my status changed from learner to researcher...*

"Just don't quit *today*!"

The next year was challenging, as I underwent radiation and faced the most challenging parts of my PhD studies. But in August 2013, I was hooded in the commencement ceremony and a month later I successfully defended my dissertation. I cannot describe the myriad emotions I experienced when I heard my mentor say, "Congratulations, Dr. Wortham!" I was overcome with joy, gratitude, relief, pride, and a host of other feelings, as evidenced by the flood of tears.

The journey to the PhD is difficult to elucidate, and I am sure that my PhD sisters can attest to this truth. Much of the PhD experience and the cancer battle is surreal, yet undeniable 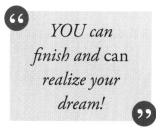 at the same time. Unexpected and unwanted events, big or small, do not have to derail you from your purpose. YOU can finish and realize your dream! My husband often reminds me of the time when he was discouraged during his master's program and shared feelings of wanting to quit. After listening and trying to encourage him as best I could, I finally said, "Honey, just don't quit *today*. Wait until tomorrow." Instead of quitting, he pressed forward and is now pursuing his doctorate. For those who feel discouraged, I offer that same word to you, "Postpone quitting until tomorrow and tomorrow..." Pause; change directions if you must, but never quit!

ABOUT THE EDITOR

Amina Abdullah, PhD, is the Program Lead for the Human Services program at Saint Leo University's Newport News Center in Virginia. She holds a PhD in human services from Capella University. Dr. Abdullah has over 20 years of combined practical experience as a human services professional from positions held in academia, telecommunications, health care, and health insurance. In addition, she serves on the board as the State Representative at Large for Virginia with the Southern Organization for Human Services, is the President of the International PhD Sisters Association (IPSA), and is the founder of the PhD Sisters Support Group on Facebook as well as the Pi Eta Delta Sorority. She also assists Custodians of Faith, a nonprofit 501(c)(3), with program initiatives, marketing, branding, and volunteering. She is a published author of the series "Their Journey to the PhD", a collection of stories from individuals who earned a doctoral degree. She is committed to advocating for and empowering young women.

The PhD Sisters Group (The Sisterhood) is the original support group open to all women who are completing or who have completed their PhD/doctoral program. The Sisterhood includes more than 900 members who engage in discussions about the PhD process, strategies for completing the program, and balancing life in terms of home, work, family, and school. For more information about the group, visit www.pietadelta.com.

Made in the USA
Lexington, KY
04 December 2014